Eyes Of Wonder

Jim Inkster

Copyright © 2013 Jim Inkster

Published by 5 Smooth Stones
The right of Jim Inkster to be identified as the authors of the
Work has been asserted by them in accordance with the
Copyright, Designs and Patents Act 1988 All rights reserved. No
part of this publication may be reproduced, stored in a retrieval
system, or transmitted, in any form or by any means without the
prior permission of the publisher, nor be otherwise circulated in
any form of binding or cover other than that in which it is
published and without a similar condition being imposed on the
subsequent purchaser.

Kelowna, BC
Canada

All rights reserved.

ISBN: 0956334245
ISBN-13: 978-0-9563342-4-4

DEDICATION

To my wonderful children and grandchildren who have filled me with inspiration over the years. I love you all dearly.

CONTENTS

	Acknowledgments	i
1	Introduction	1
2	The Wonder	Pg 5
3	Tomatoes	Pg 9
4	Reflections in the Stance	Pg 13
5	Ears Wide Open	Pg 15
6	Love in their Eyes	Pg 17
7	Through Another's Eyes	Pg 19
8	Eyes of Realization	Pg 21
9	Zooming	Pg 23
10	Big Shoes to Fill	Pg 25
11	Eyes of Expectation	Pg 29
12	Imagination That!	Pg 33
13	Defending Angels	Pg 37
14	What's Up With That, Grumpa?	Pg 41
15	Granddaughter's Wisdom	Pg 45
16	Out of the Mouths of Babes	Pg 49
17	The Bully	Pg 53

18	My Imaginary Friend	Pg 57
19	Running Backwards	Pg 61
20	Tie Breakers	Pg 65
21	I've Got Her!	Pg 69
22	A Pocket of Life	Pg 73
23	Slip Sliding	Pg 77
24	The Horse	Pg 81
25	Blackie	Pg 85
26	Gone to the Dog	Pg 89
27	The Slaughter	Pg 93
28	The Chocolates	Pg 97
29	Morning Sickness	Pg 101
30	The Race	Pg 105
31	Where's Heaven?	Pg 109
32	Help With the Puzzles, Grandpa!	Pg 113
33	Hide and Seek	Pg 117
34	Do You Like School?	Pg 121
35	Wow! Look at the Mountains!	Pg 125
36	Feminine Wiles	Pg 129
37	The Angel	Pg 133

38	Basement Baptism	Pg 137
39	Coyote - Cows	Pg 141
40	Ninja Stars	Pg 145
41	Conclusion	Pg 149

ACKNOWLEDGMENTS

I want to thank my wonderful wife, Bonnie, who has encouraged me and encouraged me over the years to write. Without her love and support I wouldn't have written anything. Thank you!

1 INTRODUCTION

Thirty some years ago my wife and I embarked on the greatest adventure of our lifetime. We had twins, a boy and a girl. Here I was a father to not just one but two. What a baptism into parenthood! Knowing that we were having two didn't prepare me any better than I was for one. I remember crying and laughing after their birth. I laughed with joy, and then cried with fear. Here goes, my big chance to screw them up. What have I done?

We had gone through all this physical preparation. We had bought cots and decorated the nursery. Bonnie and I faithfully attended prenatal classes where I diligently learned all the breathing levels so I could coach her on that laborious day. We had the bag ready for the hospital, which got more than its share of use as Bonnie did six weeks of enforced bed rest in the hospital. I had specially ordered chocolate cigars as I was not a smoker and couldn't face the idea of gagging my way through one in celebration of their birth.

But I wasn't really ready. How can you be? A doll doesn't squirm and cry unrelentingly for hours. There is nothing more terrifying than being handed a naked baby and being told to bath it. What if I drowned it? One rule, keep the head out of the water, all the rest will come natural. Oh, yeh!

Having the twins made the first six months a complete blur. Then we had the photographs professionally taken. When we got them back we were delighted with them. The one of Joel had something in it that struck me deeply. It was the look in his eyes.

I could see the wonder. The look in his eyes seemed to say to me, 'what is this place? What's that? And that? And that?' Oh, I was smitten with the wonder of their seeing things for the first time. I said to myself I must remember what they do and say. I must capture that moment for myself too.

The busyness of life didn't make it easy. But each incident that I was in tune with, made me ponder life. What do they think? How does that apply to me? At the end of the day we birth the children but we grow so much through raising them. The question sometimes is: "Who's raising who?" I changed for the better being a father. Their looks of wonder gave me a new perspective on life.

It continued through two more beautiful children. Now I also have grandchildren and get to enjoy the world through their eyes once more. Whenever I am with the grandchildren, I learn something new and fresh about the world around me. It's the fact they are seeing many things for the first time. It helps me see things anew and to not take them for granted.

Thirty years after the first photograph captured the wonder I was out with my son's son. He wasn't yet two but I saw that look of wonder in his eyes when the Christmas lights came on. The awe and the joy! Nothing was missed, nothing! It was like déjà vu as he is the spitting image of his father. The big blue eyes sparkling with delight. It inspired me to write the incidents and subsequent philosophical musings of a father and a grandfather down.

You can start anywhere in the book. Every chapter is its own incident and thought. My hope is it will cause you to chuckle and enjoy the things kids do. I also hope my thoughts will give you pause to think and reflect on life. You don't have to agree with my conclusions but please allow them to inspire your own perspective on life. Ultimately I hope the chapters slow you down enough to savour life rather than to have it pass through your hands like smoke. I think the prize isn't necessarily at the end of the race but is really the journey on the way to the tape.

2 THE WONDER

Recently we took our grandson, Warwick, who was almost 2 out for the day. A German Christmas market opens every December in our hometown with a carousel. We thought he would love it.

He was really unsure of the carousel and didn't immediately embrace the idea of riding a horse on it. I kept encouraging him how much fun it would be and not to worry. I sat next to him holding him securely on the horse by stretching my arm out and grabbing the nape of his coat. It was exciting and way too fast for a merry-go-round. When it was done he was the conquering hero dismounting from his horse.

It made me think how our heavenly Father invites us on a ride that is really exciting and we get all hesitant to try it. If we protest too much, He doesn't force us to go. If we are a little reluctant, He urges us on for He knows we will love it. Just as I did with my grandson He never lets go of us. The bible says though we stumble we will not fall to the ground for He holds us up with His right hand.

Then as we were returning to the car park the Christmas lights came on. His face was one of pure delight. He didn't miss a display or light setting as we walked along the street. He appreciated every moment and every display with joy. We passed a brass ensemble playing Christmas carols. Bonnie, who was holding his hand, was going to pass by them but he pulled her back. I was called back to enjoy the moment too. He drank in the music, eyes aglow at the wonder of these three creating music from their horns. Many people flashed past as we stood listening. It was beautiful for they were skilled musicians; well worth the coins we threw into their case.

I would have missed an opportunity to appreciate something beautiful and worthy of praise if he hadn't pulled us back. As much as I like to think I stop to smell the roses along the way I really don't. I am, probably like so many others, caught up with the busyness of life. Creation shouts the reality of our God at the top of its lungs, hoping to evoke our praise. A little boy reminded me of what a great and glorious God I serve with the simple act of stopping to admire all of His creation.

James G Inkster

3 TOMATOES

My granddaughter asked me to read a book about a little girl, Lola, who wouldn't eat anything, particularly not tomatoes. As I read Belle followed along happily until I said tomato. She said no, its tomato. To understand the significance of this you need to hear it. I will try to spell it as we said it. I said in my best Canadian English 'toe-may-toe' to which she said 'toe-mat-toe'. Whenever I had to read this word used to label red, juicy fruit, she corrected me.

I wondered why she was so adamant about correcting my pronunciation. She's only 4 and the expectation is she is old enough to speak properly. She has been full time at school this year and they have talked to her parents about her language development. It occurred to me that she daily faces correction to her pronunciation. She has learned more than how to say words; she has also learned that there is a correct way to do things. Belle is only reflecting her training.

How often do we get locked into one way of doing something because the education system tells us this is the correct way to do it? We live in the UK and have hosted many visitors from North America. The one thing that makes me cringe every time is the statement that the English drive on the WRONG side of the road. They don't drive on the wrong side; they drive on the other side of the road.

When cultures come together there is often a clash due to the fact that they solved the same problem differently. Each finds comfort in their own way of doing things labeling the other as wrong. We rigidly resist even trying it some other way because we have been taught this is the right way. Who taught us? Myriads of teachers and educators have infused us with right and wrong thinking. Is it no wonder that so many of the entrepreneurs who introduce us to so much of the innovative ideas didn't pursue academic careers?

We teach what we think are facts as truth. But it isn't

always so. For an English person a crime committed on the first floor of a building is a fact and hence the truth. But a North American would say it isn't true as the first floor for them is one below what the English call the first floor. If this is true with something so simple, why would we not question other assumptions that are passed off as truth?

James G Inkster

4 REFLECTIONS IN THE STANCE

The other day while playing with two of the grandchildren it was decided that we needed to put up Warrie's tent in Belle's room. We were going to play in it, well, sort of. I was too big so I had to lie on her bed while she and Warrie filled the tent with their favourite toys, pillows and blankets. When all was ready, we were to pretend we were asleep when the light was turned out. My imitation snoring wasn't appreciated. The light was turned on and I was told off. With the next lights out Warrie started making yelping noises like coyotes. I joined him.

Belle turned on the light, stood with her hands on her hips and told us to be quiet. She couldn't sleep with all the noise we were making. Oops! (The irony is she doesn't yield to bed very willingly for her parents.) We were in trouble. When the light went out, we laid quietly waiting for the next indication of daybreak.

Belle's parents were amused - slightly, (as I told you she doesn't cooperate that well at bedtime). They wondered where she got the idea. Hmm, probably every night when she was put to bed! Children are wonderful as they mirror their parents back to them. I remember my youngest daughter at 5 years of age yelling at the car ahead of us to "move lady, get out of the way!" when the light turned green. I asked my wife where she got that. Two traffic lights later I had my answer.

The bible says we were created in the image of God. An image is what we see in the mirror – a reflection of the reality. What is my reality? I will know by looking into my reflection in my child.

5 EARS WIDE OPEN

One evening years ago I had a very disturbing phone call. The husband of one of my church members had just torn a strip of flesh off of me for the way he thought I had talked to his wife. This shocked me as I was trying to help her and ultimately him through a difficult time. Our twins were colouring at the kitchen table as I recited the conversation to Bonnie. I didn't think they were interested or listening as they were only 3 and a half. I finished with the statement that I didn't know what to do.

A little voice piped up. My son said it was easy, I should call her adult son, explain it all to him and he would take care of it. Her son with his wife and children lived next door to them. I was stunned! After a moment I said to Bonnie I think he is right, that's what I'm going to do. Her son understood and assured me that it would be ok. He confirmed at church on Sunday that all was well. Out of the mouth of babes!

My father used to say to me when I joined adult conversations that children were to be seen not heard. I know that was the common view of children in their day. I also know he learned it from his father who probably learned it from his father. This wisdom didn't help me mature as a person. How was I supposed to learn how to talk to adults if I was only to be seen? It didn't help my sense of self worth or conversely my opinion of my father.

A child's worldview is not cluttered with as many concerns and worries as an adult's. To hear, really hear, we have to have peace of mind. That comes from setting aside all the 'what ifs' and concerns so we can hear. Before we can be heard we have to listen. Listening to others creates respect. That respect gives you credibility with others so that when you speak they will listen for in their mind you have something worth listening too.

6 LOVE IN THEIR EYES

There is nothing like the look of love in a baby's eyes when they spot Daddy coming home. I remember what it was like when our children were babies. Daddy got the royal treatment. They don't light up like this for grandpa or grandma or mommy as she is usually with them all day.

My son came in while we were visiting the family. Bonnie and I were holding our twin granddaughters. As soon as they heard his voice they turned to spot him. When he came into the room their eyes lit up and beamed love. All they wanted was to be taken in Daddy's arms and cuddled. He was in a dilemma, which one do you take without disappointing the other. He sat between us and took one in each arm and kissed them. They were so happy and content to be in Daddy's arms.

I thought about how it is with our heavenly

Father. He loves us and can't wait to embrace us. But what about all the other people you ask? Just like my son did, God does for us. His arms are more than able to hold us all. He doesn't make a choice and love one before the other. He can embrace us all at once. What a delicious thought! He always has arms open wide for you. And me!

7 THROUGH ANOTHER'S EYES

When my youngest son was 5 he brought home a picture from school. He proudly gave it to me with the exclamation that it was Daddy. My wife and I oohed and aahed over it but were a little mystified by his drawing. There were two long legs and a long body with no arms. In the middle was a large circle and on the top a small semicircle. I asked him what the circle in the middle was. He said your belly button. Where was my head? He pointed to the little lump at the top. Well, where are my arms? Oh, they're behind your back.

After he went to bed we had a good chuckle over his drawing. It was his perspective of his daddy. To me it looked distorted; to him it was perfectly normal. It gave me pause for thought. How often do we think our perspective on life is correct? When was the last time I stopped to think about how others see situations?

The world is fraught with tensions and broken relationships. People are angry at one another and full of resentment. Could it be from as simple a thing as our perspective of life? Normal for me was not normal for a 5 year old. Was I right and he wrong? We were both right.

Umm! If we are both right, how do we reconcile this? Is it possible for both parties to be right? When we think we are right, we will defend our position to the death. Unfortunately we think in terms of one must be right and the other wrong if we don't agree on what we see. Could life be more of a paradox then we allow it to be? Are we trying to keep everything simple so that we don't have to think outside our boxes?

The great challenge which may be impossible to resolve is how to be right and yet acknowledge the other is right too. Even if I try, will the other person see both sides can be right? I had no problem accepting my son's perspective. There was no issue, as I didn't make it one. As his father I am confident in who I am so I didn't need to prove to the little guy that I was right and he was wrong. Maybe that is the key! If we are confident within ourselves we won't need to prove anything.

8 EYES OF REALIZATION

A wee while ago I was playing with my grandchildren. I was pretending I was a bear that was going to get them. They would run around me while I grabbed them, held them for a bit and then let them escape. The fight turned to flight as Warwick who was 2 at the time headed for the stairs. I decided to give chase. He screamed his way up the stairs past the first landing and on to the second. I wanted to keep him running so he'd sleep better later but stayed close without catching him. Suddenly he spun around saying, "You can't catch me!" I said, "I can't?" He looked at me with his big, watery blue eyes and said, "No, I'm big boy!" "Oh no", I cried, "I've got to get away from Big Boy!" I ran down the stairs with him in hot pursuit.

I was really proud of him for facing this terrifying animal chasing him. In his mind I was a bear that was going to get him. But suddenly he got the revelation of whom he was. He was Big Boy. For about 3 months when you asked him his name he said, Big Boy. His parents couldn't get him to acknowledge his own name. Big Boy meant something special to him. He could beat up his father and his grandfather with ease. He drew on that image of himself when he was cornered and most frightened.

How many times have we run from something we should have faced? Have you ever stopped fleeing long enough to realise it was all in your head? A bugaboo! An irrational made up fear! We didn't submit our taxes because we were afraid of how much we owed. We didn't apply for the job that we always wanted because they probably aren't looking for my qualifications. Didn't bother trying the river rafting because I might get hurt.

Warwick overcame because of the confidence he had in being big boy. A young lad named David defeated a giant because of his confidence in who his God said he was.

Makes you think doesn't it about how many things we are running away from that will flee if we would only confront it head on. Go on give it a try. Fear can't resist direct confrontation.

9 ZOOMING

When my youngest son was 4, we enrolled him in a nursery school. He was so competitive and couldn't wait to start school. Everyday as we drove to the school we would play Punch Buggies. This is a very sophisticated game requiring a gift of perception and finely tuned reflexes. The core element of the game is to spot an old Volkswagen Beetle or Van and yell out 'Punch Buggy Yellow or whatever color it is'. The person with the most sightings is the winner at the end of the game.

Some mornings he wasn't quite as into it as others. I would think that today is my day; I am so far ahead of him maybe I'll win. (Wonder where he got the competitiveness from?) We would only have a mile to go so, secure in my victory, I would say to him I've got 23 to your 6. His attitude always amazed me. He would say, 'Oh, yeah! Well, I'm going to zoom off the edge!" He would then buckle down, spotting Bugs everywhere that I didn't have the opportunity to see as I was driving. Inevitably he would win. Was it his ability or his attitude?

I think his attitude made all the difference in the world. He was constantly optimistic. There is nothing impossible if you set your mind to it. I'm going to zoom off the edge should be our motto in life. He proved it to me over and over again. As he has gotten older his attitude has been dampened at times by life. We sometimes remind him of his saying to encourage him when he is discouraged.

Life has a way of wearing us down. People are generally negative and see the worst in things first. But like my son we need to see that our attitude affects what we accomplish more than anything. He was not overwhelmed by the odds being against him or the probabilities of enough Volkswagens existing in that last mile to win. All he needed to know was he could zoom off the edge.

Maybe we should start a motivational company with the slogan, Zoom off the Edge!

10 BIG SHOES TO FILL

My granddaughter tried on my trainers a while ago for fun. She could sit within them. The shoes were more like boats to her. There is a saying that those are pretty big shoes to fill. It means you have to live up to other people's expectations for you. They expect you to be as good at or better than the person you are replacing.

The worst thing about these expectations is the lack of expression. Who really tells you what they expect you to do? You fumble along trying the best you can until you are brought up on the carpet for failing to fulfill an unknown expectation. People react to you out of their disappointment or hurt because you didn't live up to their expectation. Marriages are rocked by these unspoken desires. How do you fill someone's shoes if you don't know what's expected of you?

I was thinking how ominous filling someone's shoes is too. How does a little boy fill his departed father's shoes? How does a new employee deal with the stress of filling a highly honored but departing employee's shoes? People are always effusive in praise for people who are leaving or have departed. I remember being at one memorial service for a fellow in our church and the praise for his character was overwhelming. I asked the fellow next to me if we were at the right memorial. My other thought was why didn't anybody tell him this while he was still alive. It might have helped him, as the police considered his death a possible suicide.

Now here you are replacing an employee who everyone is raving about. Big shoes to fill! The thing is you don't have to fill anyone's shoes. My granddaughter doesn't have to be me. My intent and her father's intent are to bless her in all she can be. How much more our heavenly Father wants to bless us? He isn't looking for us to fill Jesus' shoes or anyone else's for that matter. All He wants is for us to all be true to who He created us to be.

Maybe we should ask people what they are expecting from us and not settle on anything less than the truth. Then we can consider if we will try to meet them or tell them to revise their thinking. It would make life so much easier.

James G Inkster

11 EYES OF EXPECTATION

When my youngest son was 4, he was so excited about school. He wanted to do what his older sister and brother were doing. We enrolled him in a nursery school that said they would teach him math and reading. The first day he was beside himself with excitement. He couldn't wait to get into the building.

When I picked him up after school, I was expecting a beaming face full of joy. Instead I was surprised by his cool response and seeming indifference. I asked him how the big day was. He said it was good. I pushed a little bit because his answer didn't have his usual enthusiasm. He said motioning with his arms in exasperation; we didn't do any mathematics or reading!

It was tough to see him experience that disappointment. His expectation had been so high that no matter what we said to create a more reasonable level of anticipation he wasn't having a bar of it. He was going to learn to add and subtract at school and that was that!

It made me remember when I started a new position as the lead person in an organization. The founder and former leader confided in us that it wasn't all it was made out to be. He gave us some advice to help transition into the new position. It turned out to be very good advice that we never took. We thought it wouldn't happen to us like that. He's jaded and cynical and needs some refreshing. We didn't learn from him, which would have been a gentle lesson. Instead we hit the wall head on and learned everything he said the hard and painful way.

Have you ever had that intense expectation and overwhelming hope in a new situation? Have you ever found that you really didn't know what you were talking about? Congratulations! You are a full-fledged member of the human race.

I now spend my life teaching others the gentle way. Do they receive it, apply it and miss a whole lot of pain? No! Why would they? It is the folly of being young. We all pass through the same stages of life. I tell them so that they know its not unusual to experience this pain when it happens, and to give them hope that others have recovered from the same situation and so will they. Pain can create compassion within us like nothing else. Compassionate people are far easier to love and live with.

Oh, by the way, I taught him how to add and subtract driving to school using the 4-lane highway as a counting tool!

James G Inkster

12 IMAGINATION THAT!

My youngest daughter had a favorite saying when she was small. From 3 to 6 years of age she would say 'imagination that, Mommy!' Jessica would play in her room with all her dolls and toys for hours. She was totally engulfed in a world of her own creation. Everything held wonder and awe to her.

We were moving from Ft. McMurray to Victoria when she was 4. It was an adventure in moving as the rental company promised. Jessica was in the car with her grandmother, mother, sister and youngest brother following the moving van. The trip south is long with little in the way of towns to pass through. The big thrill was to arrive in Edmonton. They decided to pull off the road for something to eat. As they were driving into the city Jessica declared with excitement, "Imagination that, Grandma! They have a McDonald's in Edmonton!"

Her grandmother got such a kick out of this little one's surprise over Edmonton having a McDonald's that she told the story over and over again. Something that had become common to me was a source of such joy for her. It made me stop and think.

How could I let something so profound as Jessica's discovery of life be consumed in the routine of life? Here she was not just on an adventure in moving but in the adventure of life. She wasn't missing any of it.

That night I looked at my baby girl in a different light. What was she thinking? Who is this little bundle of joy? I started to see that she was gifted with the ability to see life in full living color. Nothing was grey or colorless to her. She colored in life just like she did with her coloring books. Her life was full of the possibilities of what could or should be. When she found something that delighted her it spilled out of her with all the enthusiasm she could muster. Imagination that! It was always too cute to correct the grammar and thank God we didn't.

Makes you think about how we get so busy with all the activities of life that we end up missing life and what is truly important. I was rushing from one goal to the next, one to do list to the next, one opportunity to the next. And the more I did the more I was missing. That old saying wake up and smell the coffee was the maxim that I was missing. I was rushing my life away in efforts to be a good father, provider and a success. My impatience for all the pieces to fall in place so that all my goals and objectives could be achieved was stealing my joy in the life I had surrounding me everyday.

I decided that night I would try to balance my life rightly by waking up and smelling the coffee.

James G Inkster

13 DEFENDING ANGELS

My first-born son was always very passionate about the truth and very sensitive. He still is. When he was 6, he came into the house with tears in his eyes, extremely upset. Bonnie and I hugged him and asked what had happened.

He explained to us that he and his friends had been riding bikes together when they started talking about God and angels. There were three of them together, which is never very good chemistry at the best of times. His closest friend, Cameron, was trying to impress Sterling who was older and much bigger. Sterling said there was no such thing as angels. Joel argued that there were. Cameron wanting to get into Sterling's good books took up his argument. Joel was facing down both boys over the reality of angels. He said he got so upset that he turned on Cameron, yelled 'yes there are angels' and punched him solidly in the stomach. Cameron went home crying, as did Joel.

After we calmed him down we told him that his zeal for God and angels was great but hitting people in the stomach who didn't believe was not the most effective way of changing their mind. I went with him to Cameron's house where he was in the garden with his dad. Joel apologized for hitting him in the stomach but not for defending the angels. Cameron and his father were open but shocked that someone should apologize.

When we went home he happily played with his twin sister and I nurtured a coffee pondering what had just happened. Here was a little guy who wasn't big for his age that stood up and defended what he thought was right. He did it in the face of formidable opposition. There were two of them against him. Cameron wasn't bigger than Joel but Sterling was a veritable hulk with a nasty streak to boot. He could have eaten Joel for breakfast and still been hungry.

Joel believed in something so much so that he was willing to go the distance to defend it. He was outnumbered, outweighed but not intimidated. He believed in angels enough to not think through the consequences and to launch an all out attack to preserve the truth.

When was the last time I stood up for something that I was convinced was right? Was I willing to fight for what I believed? Did I have the courage of my convictions that I wouldn't back down no matter what the size of the opposition?

The coffee was good; the pondering was even better. I honestly looked at my life in the light of those questions. I felt comfortable that I hadn't wavered from my beliefs but I had probably lost the zeal to stand head to head and toe to toe for what I believed. I think there is a time to turn away from a fight, but I also think there is a time to stand for what you believe, not be bullied nor intimidated. People may not agree with you but they will respect you for holding to what you believe. That was my decision that day.

James G Inkster

14 WHAT'S UP WITH THAT, GRUMPA?

We had been visiting the family in Dublin trying to make up months in a few days with the grandchildren. The two girls had been playing together. Rachel, the oldest, was not happy and snatched away the colored pencils and coloring book and left the room. Abby looked at me, shrugged her shoulders and said: "What's up with that, Grumpa?"

Abby had this profound way as a three year old of asking that question. She would shrug her shoulders, hold her arms out, palms up, and say, what's up with that, Grumpa? It was endearing but amazingly perceptive. She would do it with adults on the street who were acting badly or in the car when someone had been shockingly close to hitting the car. How did she know that at three?

Made me think! Children have this profound sense of what is right and what is wrong, what is just and what is unjust, and what is appropriate and what isn't. We just don't pay attention or give them credit for it. When I taught school, the playground was a trial courtroom and every dispute was an issue of law. He was wrong to do that was the prosecutor's position. The defendant was equally adamant in his claim of innocence. The dear teacher was the judge and jury. Without any credible witnesses the jury was hung and the judge was left with no decision to act upon. There was never any clemency or grace for the wrongdoer. Evidence or no evidence be damned, he's guilty of the infraction. It was exhausting.

Here was my 3-year-old granddaughter asking me the question: what's up with that, Grumpa? Abby my dear I have no idea. I can't tell you why people act badly at the moment. Mainly it's spawned, I think, by selfishness. I want what I want when I want it. If you don't play my way, I'm taking my ball and going home.

Children are expected to act that way at times and

parents are supposed to help them grow out of it. But unfortunately many don't. The toys change but the behavior doesn't. Abby's response was one of wonder and surprise, not anger or retaliation. When I have gotten angry or tried to retaliate, it has only hurt me. The person in the other car is either ignorant of my irritation or doesn't care. I am far better off to say: 'What's up with that?' and let it go!

James G Inkster

15 GRANDDAUGHTER'S WISDOM

We had the joy of treating our soon to be five years old granddaughter to a birthday surprise. I think the surprise was more for me. You've heard of chicken soup for the soul, haven't you? This was chicken soup.

On the way to the shopping center she was just bubbling with chatter. "I just want to say something about that," was her phrase all the way over to the mall. She told us all about spring. When we asked her how she knew so much, she told us with confidence that it was right because her mummy and daddy told her. I thought about Jesus saying we should have faith like a little child.

When we got into the parking lot, I drove by a spot that Bonnie pointed out in hope of getting one just a tiny bit closer. I pulled over to let the car behind past and said, "I should have taken that one. I made the same stupid mistake again." A little voice in the back said, "Oh, Grampa, you don't make mistakes. You never make mistakes. Its ok!" By this time I was backing towards the spot that I had ignored. As I was doing so, the same sweet voice said, "I'll just pray for a spot. Dear Jesus, we need a parking spot. Thank you." She then opened her eyes and said, "Are we in a parking spot? Oh, see! You just need to pray and He answers." (That was good; I think I will have another cup.)

We asked her when she would turn five. She said in 3 years. In a way I hoped it could be so. When we asked her what time her party was at, she said, "Half thirty!" We told her that was absolutely the best time for a party. She told us she knew that too.

When we bought her gift, a watch, we let her pick out three different ones as possibilities. We said that two of them were so pretty that we put one back right away. She then picked out the watch with the pink face and the diamond heart as the one she wanted. She floated on air as she wore her new watch out of the store.

It was off for a treat. We headed to Starbuck's, our kids' idea of the new McDonalds. I went the wrong way and got us lost. I hadn't heard her say she knew the way as Bonnie had at the beginning. But it wasn't a problem for her, she knew the way from anywhere in this mall as it was her mummy's favorite store. She shared her treat with us and even stopped before ingesting past the puke threshold.

On the way home I said something and she laughed and laughed. I really don't know what she found so humorous. But to my joy, she declared, "Grampa, you're so funny! You always make me laugh."

We dropped her off full of life and joy. As I walked back to the car with my beautiful wife I declared that this had been good for my soul. She gave us love through encouragement, hugs and kisses, and gifts. Oh yes, she gave me a gift too! With her grandmother's assistance she gave me a wonderful little package from the chemists, paracetamol with codeine. It's the thought that counts.

James G Inkster

16 OUT OF THE MOUTH OF BABES

We lived in a housing estate that had been considered very avant-garde when it was designed in the early 50s. All the houses were serviced by a lane to the rear of the house with the front gardens only having a pavement or walk down the center. There were many trees and walks through out the center park area. I used to ride my bike along the paths with Jared, 2, sitting in his bike seat.

As I rode along he would sing at the top of his lungs: "Hosanna, hosanna in the highest!" He was unabashed, undaunted and in perfect pitch. I, being the sophisticated adult, initially cringed at my son's melodious tones. I thought what would people think? But my insides said don't squash him let him sing. So I did. Everyday of our short summer we would ride and he would sing.

Have you ever been in that place of not saying or not doing something because you were worried about what people would think? Have you let your concerns for their unvoiced opinion stop you from being yourself?

I was not happy with my initial reaction to his freedom and unbridled charm. I thought long and hard about my fear and my hesitation to be spontaneous and unconcerned about what others thought. The first thing I realized is Jared didn't have any idea of what was proper or not. Where did I get that? Obviously our culture or education some how disapproves of such expressiveness. The second thing I realized is I was dancing to the tune of unvoiced opinions. No one had ever said to me that they were upset by someone singing out loud when they rode along. Nor did they say anything when Jared sang. How many times are we all bottled up because of something we think might be how people feel but don't actually know for sure? The third thing is my pride. Would I be so embarrassed by someone saying something to me that I wouldn't even try it? So they say something. Every author or artist knows that some people will love their work and others won't. If you allow that to stop you, you won't ever do anything.

All this inhibition does is steals our joy and love for life. It boxes us in to a world dictated by what others might or might not think. We become stilted conformists who really miss out on a huge amount of fun. I have worried far less from that summer on and had far more enjoyment in life as a result.

James G Inkster

17 THE BULLY

For a year and a half we lived on a hobby farm about 5 miles from the local elementary school. The twins used to catch the bus on the highway at our gate. There was a boy called Stephen who was in the same grade as the twins who caught the bus one stop before ours. Joel was the new kid in the class and Stephen decided to pick on him.

Everyday after school we met a teary-eyed, very unhappy young man getting off the bus. He would tell how Stephen would harass him by calling him names, threatening him physically and generally ridiculing Joel. We were distraught over this so went to see the school principal. He said that he would take care of it. Nothing changed. We went back to him and again he said he would take care of it. Again nothing changed. What could he do really? He wasn't on the bus; all he could do is tell Stephen to stop.

Having given the powers that be sufficient time to correct the situation I realized Joel was going to have to take matters into his own hands. I told him that Stephen was a bully, picking on him because he was sure Joel wouldn't fight. I told Joel that the next time they were on the bus and Stephen started his antics to put up his fists and say to him that he didn't want to fight but if he had to he would. Then if Stephen didn't stop, I told him to hit him on the end of the nose with all his might. I assured him that would be the only punch thrown and that Stephen would never bother him again.

The next day Joel came off the bus happy for the first time in weeks. He was so excited to tell us what happened. Stephen had started heckling him as soon as he got on the bus in the morning. Joel faced him with his dukes up and told him exactly what I said to say. Stephen laughed and called him some more names. Joel hit him smack on the nose so hard that he knocked Stephen onto his backside. Stephen scrambled for cover and Joel sat down. The bus driver told the principal who brought Joel to the office. The principal told Joel he wasn't supposed to fight on the bus but Joel told him his father said it was ok. We got a note to come into the office the next day.

The principal verified Joel's rendition of the story and said that we should have left it in his hands. He also felt it was unwise to counsel our child to use violence to solve a problem. I told him that we were not people who advocated violence as a solution but that we had come to him first. He couldn't rectify the situation and neither could we. The only one that could was Joel. I said I did coach him on what to do and say which gave Stephen the opportunity to back down. Then I looked him in the eye and said, "I have never been prouder of my son."

Bullies are everywhere. They are people who look for those who are gentle and sensitive and then intimidate them. Why? To get their way, to feel better about themselves or to have control over people through fear! The key is to stand up to them, not back down. If they have made it to adulthood and are still bullies, they won't like it. They are all smoke and mirrors like the wizard in the Wizard of Oz film. You don't have to hit them, you just need to stand your ground and not be intimidated. All of the bluster is just that – hot air. In fact laughing at them is quite effective. They can't cope with someone who doesn't take them seriously.

The ironic thing is Joel and Stephen became best buddies after with him spending many a weekend afternoon at our house. He just needed Joel to show him that there were boundaries and he respected that. Maybe that is the issue: we need to show them that we have boundaries and not to cross it anymore.

18 MY IMAGINARY FRIEND

Jared has a vivid imagination that was active when he was as young as 2. He had 2 imaginary friends, Michael and another friend whose name I don't remember that he played with for hours. Bonnie wasn't concerned about his friends but she did want him to clear up after they had all finished playing. She told Jared that he had to put his toys away after he was finished playing and not to leave them all over the lounge. This worked fine for a few days.

She came into the lounge to find it a total mess and no sign of Jared. Bonnie called him into the lounge and asked why he had not cleaned up after he was finished playing. He said to her: "Oh, that wasn't me! It was Michael."

Bonnie had to bite her lip to keep from smiling or laughing. She said to Jared that he would have to clean up for Michael, as he was his friend. Jared said he wouldn't cause it was Michael's mess. Bonnie turned him over her knee giving him a light swat on his behind saying: "The next time you see Michael give this to him for me. Now you clean up this mess." Jared never had Michael over to play again.

How at 2 years of age would you come up with this idea to blame it on someone else who isn't even real? I guess we read him too many books. Have you ever wanted to make someone up or something to cover for yourself? The temptation is huge! The thing is no one likes to be wrong or blamed or corrected. How many times do we make up people or situations to cover or shift the responsibilities away from ourselves?

We thought that left unchecked we would be encouraging a potentially bad habit to develop within Jared's character. Sure it was cute but when you in your teens, 20s, 30s, and beyond it isn't cute anymore. The consequences of facing up to your responsibilities maybe daunting at the time but it is far better than allowing the whole issue to escalate by blaming someone or something else. You in essence create a web of deceit by not taking the responsibility right off. Employers and clients lose respect for the person who tries to shift responsibility off on to others. Their loyalty to you may remain for a season but you have undermined their trust in your character. Good character is what people are buying and trusting. There are many people with the same skill set as you but only you can win people to you through character.

Another thought about the situation is Jared believed he was getting away with something and that it was the easier route than clearing up his toys. The result was correction that he wouldn't have got if he had only said he was sorry and then cleared up. Most of us get it backward. We think we are avoiding unpleasantness and pain by shifting the responsibility but to the contrary it only becomes worse. There seems to be a multiplier effect on the consequences if we shift responsibility rather than accept we were wrong immediately.

James G Inkster

19 RUNNING BACKWARDS

When the twins were five, I had decided to take up jogging at an indoor track. One day I decided to take Becky along with me for father-daughter bonding. I explained to her that I was going to run around the track for 20 to 30 minutes and she could follow me or rest on one of the benches when she got tired. We started off with her dutifully in tow. She lingered behind me for a while and then passed me. Aha, I thought! Now she will run out of steam and wait for me to finish.

The problem was she didn't run out of steam. She lapped me, which I thought was just enthusiasm and a lack of pace. When she lapped me again, I thought she's going to run out of steam soon. The third lapping wasn't funny and then it happened. She started running backwards in front of me talking to me. I could hardly breathe let alone talk. After a breathless while she flipped around and left me behind. I decided to quit at 20 minutes, as I couldn't handle the embarrassment of being constantly lapped by my 5 year old that kept saying 'Hi Daddy' to me as she passed. No one could have missed whose child she was.

What did I get out of that experience? Nothing! I mean how would you feel if your five year old ran circles around you for twenty minutes?

Well, I did realize that there are sports you are a natural at and those you have to really work at to survive. I was a swimmer and not a jogger. She on the other hand was a runner and not a swimmer. Here I was trying to get fit doing something I didn't really like because it was good for me. How much time do we spend in life doing things that are good for us but hating every minute of it? We need to find where we are naturals and pursue those activities.

We think that if it isn't hard to do then we aren't really working. So we come home miserable from a sport or a job that isn't natural to us thinking that's what real work takes. The people who are truly successful in life are those who have discovered their natural gifts and stayed with them.

Are you struggling at work? Maybe it's as simple as you are doing something you weren't made for. Take some time to evaluate your talents and gifts. Think about the activities you used to really enjoy, that were more like play than work because they were easy. Then be bold and courageous and make the change. The rewards will be worth it.

James G Inkster

20 TIE BREAKERS

We used to play a card game with the kids called Nerts. The game involved each person having a deck of cards, counting out a stack of ten placed face down, and then four cards face up. On 'go' you turned the first card in your stack over, then started to build sequences by placing cards on anyone of the four facing up. You threw all the aces into a common pot where anyone could put a card up on the ace. It was all about getting your stack of ten down first while putting up as many cards as you could on the aces. The first one through his or her stack called out Nerts and everyone had to stop. You got one point for every card in the middle but lost two for every card remaining in your stack. It was tense but fun.

We were playing one day with the youngest two.

Bonnie and Jared each had their own deck but Jess helped me, as she was only 5 and not quick enough to keep up. We were playing by games won instead of points. We had played six games winning two each. As our time was running out we thought the next hand would be the last and deciding round. We bantered over the tiebreaker, the big one. Who'd be the winner?

Jess got more and more agitated as we were dealing out the cards. The game began and she just wasn't into it. She pushed away from the table and then started pacing about the kitchen. We asked her what the problem was? She threw her arm across her eyes, put her head down on the kitchen counter and pronounced: "I hate tiebreakers, they really piss me off!"

The drama and the statement cracked us up, even though we didn't know where she got the word "p— s" from. She absolutely hated the tension and the pressure of the situation.

I never really enjoyed the pressure either because I hated losing so it was even more intense for me. But hey, I'm a big person; I have to handle the pressure, right? I have heard that some stress is necessary for a healthy life but too much can kill you. Jess had found her limit and wasn't about to take anymore. The reward of being the winner wasn't sufficient enough for her to continue in that situation.

At five she had the good sense to stop when it became too much in her eyes. At 30 or 40 do we have the good sense to stop when the stress isn't worth the reward? Is the level of achievement you are after worth the costs of pursuing? Is it affecting your family life, your relationship with your spouse, your health, or even your overall outlook on life?

Life is too short to let it be ruined by stress that we can alleviate by stopping to evaluate our ambitions and goals. Jess at five realized early that there was a limit to how much stress she wanted in her life. Each of us can handle different levels of stress but do we really need to maintain the level we now have or is there a better choice for us?

James G Inkster

21 I'VE GOT HER!

For a season my mother lived in an apartment on the beautiful shores of Lake Okanagan. We would visit her daily with the kids to keep her company. The building had a lovely sand beach, which was great fun for the children. One gorgeously sunny day we were all basking in the warmth as the kids played in the water.

Jared, almost 5, was in a life raft with Joel, 10, and Jess, 2 ½. They all had life jackets on in case of a tip. The boat was no more than 5 feet from the shore when it happened. Jess decided to move to the back of the boat, got up and promptly fell head first out of the boat. Bonnie was up like greased lightning running for the water. At the same time Jared grabbed her foot and held it as high out of the water as he possibly could. He yelled to Bonnie, 'Don't worry, I've got her!' He did have her but he had her upside down with her head still submerged. Bonnie whipped her out of the water none the worse for wear. In fact she is still our water baby.

A great deal of life is similar to this incident. You're in a situation in which you feel fairly secure riding the waves of life. Then without warning you can lose your balance and end up in the drink. You were only trying to make a small change when it all went dreadfully wrong. Even though you have had upheaval in your life you can still feel everything's going to be ok. You actually don't mind the adventure of being out of the boat because you like the waters you find yourself in.

The problems occur when good-hearted people try to help. They can hold you in such a way that you think rather than rescuing you they are drowning you with their good intentions. They bring up something that has no relevance to today. They remind you of what you were or how you used to handle situations. They are trying to help but in many ways they are more of a hindrance to you.

I've had friends who have wanted to help when they

have seen me fall out of the boat. I appreciate their help but I really wish they would just let go of things from the past and let me take the plunge. Rather than remind me of my past attempts at not succeeding at life, I want their support when I come up. I would appreciate them saying, 'Wow! You made a great dive out of a fall!'

James G Inkster

22 A POCKET OF LIFE

One day we were out helping the two youngest with their newspaper route. Jessica had picked up a stone along the road that she had found fascinating. She handed it to me as she took one of the papers to fold for delivery. I asked her what she wanted me to do with it. She said to put it in her pocket. I started to but she said, "Not that one, Dad!" I tried the one above it as her coat had two pockets on each side. "No, not that one. It's my tissue pocket."

I tried the lower pocket on the other side. She said that was her snack pocket. The one above it was for stones. Each pocket on her coat had a designated purpose: one for snacks, one for stones, one for tissues and one for money. You didn't dare mix them up as I found out. She actually seemed shocked by the fact that I didn't understand the strategy of the pockets. I had never given it a thought. For me anything and everything went in whatever pocket was most convenient at the time.

I was amazed that my little girl who seemed quite happy with the spontaneous and random was so organized. In her mind everything had a place and should be returned to its place.

I think many people in life are like Jess. They appear to be carefree and unconcerned about order. They don't snort and huff when things aren't done their way. They just roll with the punches and don't make a big deal out of things. But their ease of life doesn't mean they don't like things ordered.

Jess had her own way of ordering her possessions. Her pattern was different from mine and certainly would have astounded her grandmother. But it wasn't wrong, just different. It came from her perspective on life and what she had determined was important and what wasn't. She had her own values and they set the priorities to which she gave her attention.

So much of the conflict in life comes from not recognizing what is of value to another person and respecting it. We unconsciously judge everyone else through our life view. We believe everyone thinks as we do and holds the same values. If they don't conform to my values and views, then they are wrong, even stupid.

They're not. Just different!

To every problem or obstacle we face in life there is more than one answer or solution. The English drive on the left and the North Americans drive on the right side of the road. The same problem, how do you order traffic to avoid collisions, and two different but equally effective answers.

Let a little girl's pockets develop within you a greater respect for people's differences.

James G Inkster

23 SLIP SLIDING

It was the summer of the pox. The summer was incredibly lovely and warm but each child took a turn getting the chicken pox and with each one it was worse. It started with Jared, then Becky, then Jess and lastly Joel. There was a week between each one's recovery and the next one's outbreak. Each time we hoped that was the end of it. But no, it went through them all.

While we were visiting friends in Victoria, they introduced our children to the Slip and Slide. It was long piece of yellow plastic with grommets to peg it down in place and a connection for a garden hose. With a slight slope the water ran the whole length of the slip and slide. It took a bit of practice to get the slide perfected. The kids started running from the end with the hose attachment and then dived onto the plastic and slid to the other end. The initial attempts weren't pretty. More of a thud than a slide! Eventually they got the swing of it and were having a ball.

Joel loved it. He was the biggest and could slide the furthest. He also was quite sweet on one of our friend's daughters and wanted to impress her. The last slide was awesome. He took a long run, leapt onto the slide and slipped right off the end. Unfortunately, he bent his hand under his body when he first landed on the slide. He got up dancing in pain. We took him to a clinic immediately where they x-rayed the arm. It turned out to be a greenstick fracture, I think the doctor called it. More like cracking a twig than breaking it. The doctor set it in a cast and Joel was again the hero.

Unfortunately it was the summer of the pox. He was the last one to get it and his was the worse case of all. He had the pox sores everywhere including inside his cast. There was nothing we could do for those ones. We could at least apply calamine lotion to all the other exposed ones. I'm pretty sure I saw him rubbing his arm with a ruler inside the cast. He was desperate for some relief and that was the only way he could get it.

Basically he had an itch he couldn't scratch. There are times in life when we all have to endure an itch we can't scratch. There are people in positions that make your life miserable. They might be a teacher, a boss, even a friend of a friend and there is nothing you can do to alleviate the irritation. You just have to endure it until the restraint holding you in check is removed. It could be the end of term, or the friend's friend moves or you get a new boss or position. Until then all you can do is be patient.

Patience is considered a virtue. Virtue is only acquired through submitting to an unwelcome obligation or an unavoidable circumstance. Ouch! Although we develop patience through trials and testing the best way to make the most of this time is to focus on other activities or interests. If we concentrate on the situation we find ourselves in it only makes the whole thing worse. We can't speed it up, so try making the most of it by minimizing your attention on that which you can't change and maximizing your attention on what you can change.

James G Inkster

24 THE HORSE

One day while we were visiting the grandchildren I got down on all fours and pretended I was a horse. Belle climbed on my back and I crawled around the lounge. Warwick had a go at riding double and both of them kept falling off. My occasional buck or wiggle didn't help it. Warwick decided he was going to his house, which is the room off of the lounge. I kept coming up to the door and knocking on it. He would open up and tell me that I wasn't allowed in his house. Belle was still firmly gripping me with her legs and riding her horse.

I returned to the house and he wouldn't open the door. I pulled the door open with him hanging on for dear life to the other side. I was being my usual half passive – half aggressive animal. It doesn't matter whether it was a bear, horse or lion; I'm essentially the same, looking to get a reaction. He was protesting vehemently as I pulled him and the door open. Belle had had enough. She said, "No horsey, stop! If you don't, we'll have to take you to the scrap yard!" "The scrap yard!" I said, "Why the scrap yard?" Belle answered that the scrap yard was where you went when you were being bad. I told her I didn't want to go to the scrap yard and let go of Warwick and the door.

Educational television produces some interesting concepts of life. Both of them have watched Thomas the Tank Engine many times. When one of the engines misbehaves they apparently send it to the scrap yard. Neither child actually knows what a scrap yard is but they know it isn't a good place to be.

Wouldn't it be wonderful to simply send all the problem people in our life to the scrap yard? There they would be remorseful and would reform so they could re-enter our society. It would be interesting to see whom we would send over in a day. Probably all our children, most of the other people driving on the road, the person who took our parking spot, and depending on our mood virtually anyone we encounter could end up there.

But what if they had the same power as us? Would we escape the scrap yard? I doubt it; in fact, by the end of the day we would all be in the scrap yard.

Maybe there is a use for the scrap yard in our life. Instead of getting upset or angry with people we could say, "Off to the scrap yard with you!" Aw, that's better; I'm not tense or bent out of shape over what others have done. I've satisfied my judgment with their punishment and can now look forward to their reform. It could work!

James G Inkster

25 BLACKIE

When we first moved to the farm, the grandparents blessed our twins with a cat each. Becky called hers Kathleen, and Joel called his Blackie. Strangely his cat was black. They were sweet and loveable kittens when we arrived in May. The kittens hung around the house or ended up as dress-up dolls at the playhouse.

By November they were almost full-grown and wandered all over the farm. The railroad on one side and the highway on the other enclosed the farm. As convenient as the highway was for us, it was deadly for cats. Blackie went missing and a search was initiated. After awhile most of us ended up back in the kitchen having a coffee or hot chocolate to warm up. Joel and his cousin, who were searching together, burst into the house.

"We found Blackie," they shouted. But the look on their faces told us it was not going to be a time of rejoicing. Joel had tears in his eyes and could hardly speak. He said that they found him dead in one of the culverts under the driveway from the highway. Tom said as dramatically as he could, "This is the worst day of my whole life!"

We embraced them and let them have a good cry to express their sorrow. I scooped Blackie up with a shovel and we buried him in the garden with a full service. The next day Joel and Tommy were off on another adventure around the farm.

Life is full of disappointments and heartaches. No one is immune from them. We will encounter days that at the time seem the absolute worst day of our life. In the moment I think I will never forget what this feels like as long as I live. Sincerely I believe the boys felt that it was their worst day. The next day you would never have known it had happened. They had too much life to live to abide there.

When unpleasant and unwanted situations occur, we have to embrace our feelings and grief, allowing them to be expressed, as we will. In time as time has a way of easing the pain things improve. Do you forget what happened? No, you just mustn't dwell there. Life moves on.

As the boys showed me, there is always hope for a new day and a new adventure.

James G Inkster

26 GONE TO THE DOG

Living on the farm we had a lovely Blue Heeler – sheep dog cross, called Jackie. She had a thick white coat and was as tall as Jared when he was 3. Jackie had a voracious appetite and ate everything insight including one of our two pet rabbits. She had the other one cornered under the car when we rescued it. If anything stayed still long enough she would eat it.

I fed her dry dog food in a large hubcap once a day. The bag weighed 25 kg (50 lb.) bag. She always devoured the food immediately, not even pausing long enough to breathe. We noticed that Jackie was getting larger and larger around the girth. I checked with Bonnie's parents to see if I was feeding her too much as she was initially their dog before they left the farm. They said that one hubcap a day was all she needed. It was a mystery, as I didn't think she could catch that many mice to add to her waist so significantly. She looked like a pear when she sat.

One morning after I had fed her I was working in the yard on the forklift closer to the house. I saw Jackie hustle over to her bowl with great anticipation. This caught my attention. As I watched I saw this little tyke, Jared, pulling an almost full bag of dog food through the door. He somehow managed to tip it over the hubcap bowl and the food would overflow the lip. The dog leapt on the food as Jared pulled the bag back into the house. Suddenly things were clear. He had watched me do it and wanted to be like me. So every morning he fed her a second bowl of food to her great delight. It took months for her to work off that extra portion but our dog food bill dropped significantly.

How can you be upset when your son only wants to be like you? Imitation is the most sincere form of a compliment. He saw something in what I was doing and he wanted to be like that. I was flattered.

Often in life we are imitated but mistake it for something other than a compliment. I know I have been upset because I thought other people were trying to gain promotion by using my ideas or methods. I would even think that they weren't treating me seriously enough because they would do what I would do but some times tease me with it. I truly didn't understand what an impact I was having on people. I imitated my father and other people I admired yet never realized what it was when it happened to me.

If people can imitate you, it means they have watched you closely. You don't watch people who are insignificant to you. But you do imitate those who have left an impression upon you.

I wonder if some of the conflict that occurs in the workplace or within relationships is simply a failure to recognize a true compliment from those who are impacted by us?

27 THE SLAUGHTER

On the farm we had two beef cows that were due for the table. We knew that Grandpa was getting eager to bring them to the butcher's but we never suspected that he would chose Thanksgiving as the day to put them down. We had invited family and friends to come for dinner that Sunday afternoon.

The next thing we know Grandpa has his rifles, a 30-30 and a 22, out. I asked him what was up. He said we're going to kill the cows, gut, skin, and hang them in the barn. I was stunned. Today when company is coming over I said. You betcha, he said. It would be a waste to have all that help around and not make use of it. I thought he was kidding but I was wrong.

The cattle were grazing in the pasture between the house and the highway. When Grandpa and his son went out to shoot the animals, all the children ranging from 3 to 9 years of age surrounded them. I suggested it might be a bit traumatic for them to see the animals shot right before them. I certainly didn't want to be spending the night consoling my children after they saw what happened. On this he agreed with me and we sent the children down to the north end of the property to play.

With their departure the execution commenced. It wasn't pretty as they missed the beasts a number of times. In the midst of the shooting I heard little excited voices giving a running commentary on what was happening. I looked to the north end of the property and there were the children all standing on a knoll which gave them a spectacular view of the whole event.

It was too late to do anything about their participation in the event. I talked to them after in trepidation that they may have been traumatized by the whole affair. They weren't fazed in the least by the whole process. I realized that children raised on the farm were far more aware and less delicate about the life of an animal bred for food.

I had been raised in the city with no pets. My view of farm life, and animals in general, had been shaped by a gentleman called Walt Disney. I loved his show and never missed it. He had a wonderful way of giving animals human characteristics and personalities. It really warped my perceptions of farm animals. Although I had worked with the cattle and chickens, this imagery was deeply engrained. My worldview shaped by television was affecting my perceptions of the real world. The chickens were not capable of having deep and meaningful conversations together. They were only concerned about eating. The cows weren't smart enough to know better than to defecate in their own food.

Here I was on a farm imposing my Disney life view on everyone else. They knew what the cows were for and they weren't harmed by the inevitable. It brought my life foundations under new scrutiny. I know that my perception of the intelligence of the animals or their character is not a life-changing revelation. But it does make me wonder how many other misconceptions we believed as young children are haunting the decisions of our adult life and skewing our interpretation of events happening around us? Hmmm!

James G Inkster

28 THE CHOCOLATES

When Joel and Becky were about six, we had given them some individually wrapped chocolates. The day after I noticed Joel was asking Becky for a chocolate, which she gave him. I asked him where his were. He informed me that he had eaten them all. I was astounded.

It was time for the "wisdom" talk. I explained to him that it wasn't fair to Becky that he ate all of his candies and then asked her for some of hers. He was getting more then. She was showing wisdom and self-discipline by eating only a few at a time. He promised to reform his ways. At Easter we hid small chocolate eggs all around the house for them to find. They both had an equal amount at the end of their foraging. Joel announced that he was going to eat two and put the rest in a safe place so that he could have some the next day. We thoroughly encouraged his change of habit with abundant praise. He glowed in the midst of all the acclamation.

A couple of days later I saw him asking Becky for one of her chocolate eggs. I said to him that I thought he was saving them and not eating them all at once anymore. He informed me that he was saving them and he hadn't eaten them all. I asked why he was asking Becky for an egg then. He looked kind of sheepish and announced that he had hidden them so well he couldn't find them.

I think that our wisdom sometimes is shaped more by our values than true insight. My values of "what is fair" and "what is proper use of resources" skewed my wisdom. Those who hold the same values will agree with me, and those who don't hold those values will disagree with me. One will say that's wise; the other will say it's about time you realized you're not that wise.

The wise thing to have done was to accept that Joel and Becky are different. For her there was great satisfaction in eating some of them everyday. She also loved to share and wasn't bothered by her brother's requests for some of her chocolates. This is her nature. He on the other hand enjoyed eating them all at once. He would share with her when he had some but often she was the one with something and his was gone. He had an outlook on life that said I'll enjoy today for today and see what tomorrow brings. She enjoyed today but found satisfaction in saving something for tomorrow. Who's the wiser? Does it matter? They both were happy the way they were. He never complained when his candies were gone and she never complained when she was asked to share.

So in our wisdom has it ever occurred to us that we would essentially create one bland homogenous world with no variation or differences? How dull that would be!

By the way, we never did find the chocolates. We think he must have hid them in a heating duct and that they slid down out of sight and reach. What a waste!

James G Inkster

29 MORNING SICKNESS

Jared was 18 months old when Bonnie became pregnant with his sister. As in all the pregnancies she suffered morning sickness for the first 3 months. Often her routine was to prepare breakfast for the three children and see the older two off to school. She would then go to our bathroom, lift the lid and throw up.

Jared followed her everywhere. Soon he began to imitate her. He would stand next to her at the toilet and make heaving noises too. Then she flushed the toilet, brushed her teeth, and he followed her out. After the first 3 months she stopped having the nausea. Jared who had fallen into the routine was a little mystified why mommy didn't go to the bathroom as per routine. But unfazed by her lack of participation he went to the toilet, lifted the lid, made retching noises, put the lid down and flushed the toilet. He suffered morning sickness a whole week longer than Bonnie.

I have said that imitation is one of the most sincere forms of a compliment. In this case I don't think so. The difference between imitation as a compliment or not is in the understanding. If someone understands what you have done or said and then imitates you, it is a compliment. But if someone simply apes your actions, it isn't a compliment. But it does speak of our human nature. One person can admire someone so much they want to be like them in all they do. They can take on mannerisms and actions with little or no understanding of how or why they are performed.

In any position of leadership or authority we can have people who come under our influence who admire us so much that they mimic our behavior. To allow that pattern to continue when we have the right to address it is unwise. We may think that it is great that they are doing things just the way we would. But if they don't have any understanding they can cause a great deal of damage and conflict that is unnecessary. They will carry the same response into every situation because that's what they think you would do. The problem is there is no one set answer or response for every situation.

It is easier to work with people who act just like you do than to deal with people who might question what you are doing. But after awhile the whole organization or structure can be ineffective because people are responding not out of understanding but out of rote learning. If parameters change in situations, they can't.

Jared took a week but realized it's over. How many adults are unconsciously repeating and repeating behavior that is no longer necessary or relevant?

James G Inkster

30 THE RACE

Every year in June Canadian schools participate in a ritual that is a joy for some, a dread for others and a pain in the backside for teachers and staff. That's right – track and field day! There was one particularly memorable one for me. The twins were 9. Bonnie and I were there encouraging them on in all their different events.

The time came for the girls' 200-metre race. Remember it wasn't a run but a race. With the starter pistol's bang 20 nine year old girls hurled themselves down the track. Becky was a natural runner and very fast. She was well out in front with less than 30 metres to go. Her friend, Tracy, was 30 metres behind. Suddenly Becky started to slow down. Tracy chugged and puffed towards her in an effort to overtake Becky. I was yelling at the top of my lungs, "Go, Becky, Go!" She ignored me and slowed even more. Within 5 metres from the finish line Tracy passed her and threw herself through the ribbon. Becky glided in to take second place. I was incensed, beside myself with shock that she had given up and let this other girl win. It was so obvious that she let her win. Arrgh!

I kept up the pretense that all was fine and how good it was to win second. Tracy was waving the trophy around and gloating about her win. I really, really wanted to stick that trophy somewhere unmentionable, really. My wife and daughter didn't seem to even notice, which was all the more maddening.

When we were home having dinner, I asked Becky why she slowed down. "Oh", she said, "I heard Tracy calling me and I knew she wanted to win badly so I slowed down to let her". "You what? Didn't you want to win?" I asked. "No, it doesn't matter to me like it does to her."

I was so, …so, …so upset. I kept my cool. Even if I didn't hide it that well, it didn't intimidate Becky into being anymore aggressive in sports. She liked to play, winning was incidental to her.

I hated track and field days when I was in school. Oh, was I competitive? Terribly, but unfortunately, if I didn't think I could win, I wouldn't enter the race. I hated to lose. But I had also come to believe when I was in grade two that I didn't have the ability to compete in athletics. So, I dreaded the day. For me it was a "lose – lose" situation. I hated the whole day.

Here I was 30 years later with a daughter who could run circles around me and she didn't care if she won or not. I was looking for redemption for my own failings through her. I wanted to satisfy my competitive nature through her. Fortunately she wasn't having a bar of it as she took after her mother who loves to play but doesn't care if she wins or not. That is a mindset that competitive people will never understand.

The saddest thing is I believed a lie that I couldn't win so why try. I will never know if with practice and a right mental attitude, what I could have done.

Worst yet, I could have pushed and coerced Becky into trying to fulfill my unfulfilled ambitions. It might have made me happy in some weird way but it wouldn't have been right for her. Kind of makes you wonder how many people are laboring under their parent's unfulfilled aspirations?

31 WHERE'S HEAVEN?

My son, Joel, was telling me about his daughter's obsession with Jesus and the cross. She had her first religious education class and the speaker, as it was Lent, spoke on the topic of Christ, His death and His resurrection. Annabelle never got passed the death on the cross. After days of reading that portion of the story to her Joel was trying to get her to think about other things spiritually.

During their bedtime ritual he was asking her a number of questions about God. She had been holding a takeaway menu from a Chinese restaurant in her hands while they were talking. Joel asked her where heaven was? He knew she was tired but thought he would try this one question. She hesitated for a bit, flipped open the menu to the page that had a location diagram, and said, "Straight on at the roundabout, Daddy!"

With that he tucked her in and kissed her good night.

Even the best-phrased question can be misunderstood. I remember being in a buffet restaurant with my wife and a friend. The restaurant was playing music softly over their sound system, which caught my attention. Bonnie was already at the table eating her dessert when I asked my friend if that was Nana Mouskouri? Before she could answer Bonnie said, "I don't know but it sure is good!" We cracked up as she thought we were talking about the dessert not the singer.

Belle's answer was totally credible with her level of understanding. Because she didn't give what we think is the correct answer, is she stupid? No! No! No! She is a very intelligent little girl. The question simply asked her something that was outside her frame of reference. My question was outside my wife's frame of reference. Bonnie has never followed the celebrity scene although she loves music and movies. Just don't ask her titles or names. She doesn't know or care.

One professor I had said that questions determine the level of intelligence of the person asking. If we think that someone isn't very bright because they didn't answer the question the way we expected, we are probably sadly mistaken. The answer often reflects on the quality of thought put into the question.

Even so, Bonnie wasn't looking at the visual clues in our conversation as she was so wrapped up in her food.

James G Inkster

32 HELP WITH THE PUZZLES, GRANDPA!

When my granddaughter, Rachel, was 4 to 5 years old she used to ask me to help her with her puzzles. She had one that was particularly intriguing as it had several jigsaw puzzles in a book format. Rachel would flip open a page, shake out the pieces and ask me to help put them back. As I would take a piece and try to fit it in place she would push my hand away and place her own. After a number of attempts I would stop trying. She was quite good at subtly blocking my efforts.

I would get exasperated and stop. I know, I know, I'm the adult, I'm supposed to be above this. After all she's only a child. I totally realized that but it didn't make it any less frustrating. I wouldn't have minded if when I stopped she just contentedly continued placing the pieces. But instead she would then look at me and say, "Why aren't you helping me, Grandpa?" I would tell her that she keeps blocking my attempts to help her. She would promise me that she wouldn't do it again. Within one piece of restarting the puzzle she would again be blocking my hand.

Human nature doesn't change much between 5 and adulthood. Have you ever been asked to help someone who is struggling with a difficulty in his or her life but every attempt you make is brushed aside? I think this is particularly common for those who work in the caring careers. People come to you asking for your expertise and then ignore what you say.

I remember one particular occasion where a family were having trouble handling their four young boys. My wife, Bonnie, was asked if she would help. Bonnie agreed to spend some time talking to the mother about the situation. After listening to the mother download the situation to her, Bonnie started to make suggestions of possible solutions to the problem. With each attempt she put forth the mother said, "Oh, we tried that but it didn't work." After an hour of having her hand brushed aside Bonnie said to her that she was sorry but she had no further ideas that might alleviate the situation.

A while back I was conversing with a young person about what we were hoping to do. She looked at me and said, "You have a lot of problems asking for help, don't you?" I said I did. But it made me think: is it better to ask for help and keep brushing people's hands aside or is it wiser not to ask at all?

My choice is not to ask if I don't want to do what they might suggest. As one receiving requests I have become more and more wary of the level of sincerity of the askers. But how many of us don't realize that our hands are being brushed aside and keep wasting our time giving answers that aren't being received?

James G Inkster

33 HIDE AND SEEK

Warwick at 3 wanted me to play hide and seek with him. We were upstairs in his room when he made the suggestion. He said he would count and I could hide in his room. His room was about 8' by 8' with a wardrobe in the corner. So I hid behind the door. When he opened it to seek me, I would be hopefully hidden by the door.

He finished counting a random assortment of numbers and announced he was coming whether I was ready or not. He pushed open the door and found me immediately. No surprise, really!

He looked at me with a wrinkled brow and said, "Grandpa, that's not good enough!"

"Not good enough?" I asked.

"No, not good enough. Here!" he said and pushed me into the wardrobe. "That's better." And he left the room to count. Imagine his surprise when he found me hiding in his wardrobe. After 5 games he decided we would do something else and let me out of the wardrobe.

How many of us are stuck in small places? Our options are limited and we are just trying to get by. It might not be as small as his room but we just find we have nowhere to go. Do we then become small in our minds and limit ourselves to the size of our present situation?

Warwick demanded more of me than I had given. He felt that there was more potential in the situation than I had seen. I think that in any situation there is more potential than we think. We need to expect more and turn a wardrobe into a quality-hiding place. Instead of looking at something from the most obvious perspective lets turn it on its head. There is always more than one possibility in every situation.

The key is in our attitude. In hide and seek terms I just wasn't good enough. With a little effort I became a star, fitting into a wardrobe that I never thought would hold me. When I played above and beyond what I could see, I was released from the small place.

Maybe the small place you find yourself in will become expansive if you change your perspective through changing your attitude.

James G Inkster

34 DO YOU LIKE SCHOOL?

Jessica had a friend over for a Saturday playtime. She and I drove her friend home. On the way conversation centered on school and Jessica's comments were twigging thoughts I had been having about her education. She was in the back seat when I asked her the question. I can still see her in blue tights and a horizontally stripped blue and pink dress.

"Jessica, do you like school?" She wriggled around and finally said, "Yeah! Sort of!" Her answer definitely lacked conviction or sincerity. I asked her again. She squirmed some more obviously uncomfortable with the line of questioning. She said, "Well, Daddy, you have too!" I asked why did she have too? She said, "Because it's the thing you do between the weekends."

That left me a little speechless.

Jess was never one to complain and always tried to see the best in every situation. Even with that attitude school really wasn't a joy for her. I think there are many, many people who are in careers and employment that like Jessica would say, "work is what you have to do Monday to Friday". They may be putting on a brave face and trying not to complain but deep down inside they are simply surviving.

My brother told me about some advice he received when he was in a very difficult career situation. Basically it was that we labor under the idea that work has to be hard to be truly genuine work. If we find it easy and enjoyable we can't possibly be working. So we settle for something that we may even be good at but not great at as it isn't what we are gifted to do. We are working hard, not enjoying it, but it must be right since it's hard. The advice was to do what we are great at, that which is natural and comes easy to us. If we do, we will find pleasure in our work and we will achieve more successfully.

My brother went back into sales and excelled. We took Jessica out of school and home schooled her. She loved the change, read and read and read, which brought up her reading level, and subsequently excelled in her studies. This adjustment to her schooling changed her attitude and desires towards education to the point she enrolled in and graduated from university. If we had left her in the school, she would eventually have hated learning, as it did not suit her learning style.

Are you doing what you are gifted to do? Or are you ignoring your gifts and talents to do something that you think must be right since it's hard? In a leadership college I gave the students a survey on their motivational gifts. One of the students who snorted the most over doing the survey actually realized that her motivational gifts were incompatible with her career. At the end of the course she retrained and found a new job that she enjoyed doing.

Why live for the weekends only? The pleasure in flowing in your gifts and talents is well worth making the changes necessary to be in the right career.

James G Inkster

35 WOW! LOOK AT THE MOUNTAINS!

We have had family and friends living in British Columbia all of our married life. It was important in our minds to take the children to see their family and equally to give them as much exposure to travel and new experiences. We felt as teachers who had taken a course in child development that this was essential to their education.

We had driven through the mountains at least once a year for their entire life not to mention having lived in BC for four years as well. The oldest two were 11 when we made a trip from Alberta to Vancouver Island on the west coast. Essentially we were driving through all the mountain ranges in the province on our route. We were just passing through the Roger's

Pass in the Rockies when Joel and Becky who were riding in the back of the van looked out the window and started shouting, "Wow! Look at those mountains, and all the waterfalls. Where did they come from?"

We were stunned. We asked them what they were so excited about thinking we must have misinterpreted what they said. They said the mountains. They were amazed at how beautiful they were and how huge. It still didn't register as they had been through them every year of their life for the past eleven years. As we questioned them it became obvious that it was the very first time they had really seen them. Wow! We were stunned. I realized the true value of the private school we had been sending them to.

I was disappointed, as it seemed all the effort we had put into providing our children with rich stimulus and exposure to many different experiences had been futile. What a waste I thought! But I changed my mind as I thought about it. We are surrounded with so much stimulation: TV, billboards, radio, cinema and the local environs as well. If anything, the problem is over stimulation. They had seen so much that it couldn't all be assimilated.

When you think that everything in a child's life is virtually seen for the first time, how much can they retain? They and we are bound to miss something along the way. The kids were travelling hundreds of miles at a time and they could only register so much without blowing a mind gasket.

Have you ever had the experience of noticing something for the first time that you are sure wasn't there before, only to have someone say that was always there? It's exciting to think that you haven't seen it all. The adage: "been there, done that, bought the tee-shirt" doesn't have to apply to our life. There is always something new to see and experience. It's up to us to keep open to seeing things for the first time. Rather than curl up, wander down memory lane and wait to die, we can look for all the wonderful vistas and experiences we have missed so far. Life is for the living!

James G Inkster

36 FEMININE WILES

When the twins were two, we were out for a walk around the neighborhood. As we came along one street there was a young lad of 4, maybe 5, riding a hot wheel tricycle in his family's driveway and out into the street. He stopped when we passed by, all eyes upon Becky. He left his bike and ran passed us where he waited for us. He stared at Becky who totally ignored him.

Then the most amazing thing happened. When she got past him, she looked over her shoulder and smiled. His face lit up and he ran past us again. She ignored him completely. His face collapsed. Ten feet past him she looked over her shoulder again and smiled. He sprung to his feet, roared past, did a somersault and lay on his back looking up at her.

Becky ignored him. He was crestfallen. Ten feet past she smiled again. Bam! He was up on his feet, running passed us, and then showing off in some attempt at acrobatics. She did it again. Blanked him completely. He was the picture of heartbreak and despair. Ten feet further, you guessed it, over the shoulder smile. She would give him the come hither look and he was putty in her hands.

This occurred over and over again along his street and the one we turned off onto. Bonnie and I were getting really concerned that his parents would be wondering what happened to him. We had to pick Becky up, tell her to stop leading him on, and shoo him away like a stray puppy we didn't want following us home. Two years old and she had an older man completely twisted around her finger! Wow!

In the movie, My Big Fat Greek Wedding, the mother tells the daughter the man maybe the head but the wife is the neck and we can turn him anyway we want. Solomon in Proverbs said there were four things he did not understand, one of which was the way of a man with a maiden. Women have the capacity to reduce the strongest man to a sniffling, out of control fool. For her attention he will do anything.

At two Becky had the ability to make this boy dance to her tune. She never said a word; she just knew when to look, when not too, and when to smile. I have heard many of the young ladies say that the men seem to be so clueless today. They give them their best hints and they miss them. I can't judge the quality of their come-ons but I know a two year old had the ability to wind a 5 year old around her finger. I also know that girls have given up on subtle and have become simply forward, asking the boy out instead of waiting. Hmm!

Doesn't a man need the sense that he is the pursuer? Doesn't his ego require that affirmation that he swept her off her feet? My wife always tells the young ladies that she ran away just fast enough for me to catch her. Have we lost the art of the subtle and the sublime in the west? I know I thought I won my wife; she knows she let me.

37 THE ANGEL

We never let the children sleep through the night with us but it was common for them to come in early and climb into bed. I usually slept like a log so I was always surprised whom I would find in bed when I woke up. One morning when Jess was 8 she slipped into bed.

It was a lovely spring day with the sunlight beaming into the room. Jess had just snuggled in when she asked who the man was in the room. I looked around, shocked that some stranger should be in our room. There was no one. We asked her if she could see a man? She said, "Yes. Up there by the ceiling in the corner." Bonnie and I both looked to where she was pointing. Neither of us saw a man.

"Are you sure you see someone?"

"Oh, yes!"

"What does he look like?"

"Well, he has on green tights, a short brown jacket, brown pointed hat, longish hair, a thing with arrows over his shoulder and a bow in his hand."

"Does he scare you?"

"Oh, no! Not at all!"

"Well, that's good then. We'll just let him stay, shall we?"

"Sure!" And she changed the subject to what's for breakfast.

So, is it a case of an overactive imagination? Did she watch too much TV? Was it real? Did she see something that we couldn't? Why not?

There is a great deal of interest in paranormal phenomena today. People are seeking mediums and attending séances. There are tours and TV shows devoted to the subject. Horoscopes are a part of people's everyday rituals. Harry Potter sold millions. All of this in scientific, rationalistic, western societies!

The church has a history laden with stories of angels and demons. The bible talks of angels. It is not something to be ignored. Our daughter had been sensitive to spiritual things from a very early age. She was able to tell you whether it was safe or something fearful. We rested in the fact that the man by the ceiling was an angel sent to protect us, as she was very much at peace with his presence.

Interestingly, that was the last one she mentioned and for years now she hasn't seen anything. Why? We didn't discourage her. What blocked her capacity to see in this realm? Was it school and science, or the influence of her peers who didn't see and couldn't understand? She doesn't really know why; she just knows she doesn't see them anymore.

Years ago there was the disaster at Chernobyl when the nuclear reactor melted down. The scientists denied there was a problem when they were contacted as all their instruments in the control room indicated everything was normal. They even went outside amongst the glowing chunks of nuclear fuel and could not see the disaster all because their instruments told them everything was fine. They continued to deny there was a problem to the point of their own death by radiation poisoning. Why? Because their minds had no ability to see beyond what they were convinced was right.

Tragically people interpret their surroundings not by what they see but by what they believe. If they believe it can happen, they can see it when it does. But if they are convinced it can't be, they will miss it completely when the evidence is flagrantly in their face. We believe what we want to see is real, not always what is real.

38 BASEMENT BAPTISM

When Joel and Becky were 4, we had bought a new fridge and stove which came in the most wonderful cardboard boxes. We set them up in the family room in the basement for them to use as houses, forts or whatever else their imagination could come up with. One day a friend was over with her two daughters, 3 and 2. The kids went off to play while we had coffee in the kitchen.

Soon we could hear singing coming from the basement. They were having a church service. We heard the singing, and then it stopped. Next we heard Joel, at the top of his voice, pronounce over Jenny, "I baptize you in the name of the Father, the Son and the Holy Ghost, that name that is above all names, the name of Jesus Christ." There were noises from feet on cardboard and then cheering. We had to look. They had turned one of the boxes on its side so the opening faced up and were using it as a baptism tank. Joel was the minister, Becky the worship leader, Jenny the convert getting baptized and Rachel the congregation.

As you might have guessed I was a minister. Their play was really enlightening. They had a baptism service down to a tee. They knew what to do, what to say and when to say it. But if you had attended a service with them you would have thought they weren't paying any attention to what was going on. They would look completely disinterested, bored or occupied with something else like coloring or talking or playing with toys. Yet they had even the nuances of voice perfectly imitated. Jenny sounded like she really needed God to come into her life.

If you have had the pleasure of public speaking (also considered to be the most feared activity in life, even more than death), you will know how disinterested people appear to be in regard to what you are saying. They look at the floor, scour the ceiling, and occasionally glance at you. I have often thought in the middle of a speech, 'what am I doing here? No one's listening!' I have even tried to bring it to a quick conclusion. On one occasion the hall was like a tomb, it was so quiet. I looked down at my notes to see if I could conclude this message with some coherence and get out of there. I couldn't so I kept on. I was amazed at the positive response after I finished. (No, it wasn't just because I was finished!)

One woman used to come to our church and while I was speaking she sat with her arms folded across her chest staring at me. I interpreted her body posture as she was closed to anything I had to say and was just tolerating this part of the meeting. I used to wonder why she kept coming to the church if she didn't like the messages. At a party she told me that when she attended school in Holland before moving to North America, they taught the students to put down their work, pens and pencils and to cross their arms over their chest so that they would not be distracted from what the teacher was saying. She told me that she always did this when I spoke so she wouldn't miss anything I had to say. Wow! Talk about a completely opposite and erroneous interpretation of her body language. She was honoring me by putting aside anything that could distract her and I thought she was resisting everything I said.

So, what am I thinking about all this? I think we need

to realize people are far more attentive than we think. Reading body positioning can be helpful but not always. If we depend on it too much, we will be wrong more often than right in interpreting what is being said. The other night at a concert I had closed my eyes to visualize the music the strings ensemble were playing. I felt a sharp piercing pain in my thigh as my darling wife interpreted my closed eyes to be a state of slumber overcoming me. Even though we get it right occasionally, doesn't mean we are going to be right every time. We need to judge each situation on its own merit.

39 COYOTE-COWS

We moved to Bonnie's parent's hobby farm when the children were 8, 3 and 3 months old. The farm consisted of 10 acres in a diamond shape framed by the highway and the train line. On the hills at the back of the property a rancher had a fair herd of cattle. It was May and the cows were in heat. They would bellow for their lover and the bulls would bellow back, 'I'm coming, honey!'

In the midst of this cacophony of noise there were the coyotes that had been raiding the pigeon and chicken coop. They would bay but rarely. All of this wildlife and nature was new to my city-raised family. The thieving coyotes were the focus of Grandpa's concern. Jared, 3, listened intently to all his ranting and then Grandpa pointed out the dulcet tones of the sneaky devils. At this point we all ran out into the yard towards the chicken coop.

Jared was very excited. Every time a cow would bellow he would say, "Listen, coyotes!" We tried to correct him by telling him that it was the cows. He wouldn't believe us or rather wouldn't concede that he could be wrong. He kept saying it was the coyotes. We were trying to teach him the difference between the sound of cows and the howl of coyotes. Suddenly, he stopped after one of the cows let out another bellow. He looked very intently at us and said, "It's coyote-cows! Listen to the coyote-cows!"

Hmm! What did I learn from my little fellow that day? Well, no matter how young you are, no one likes to be wrong. I haven't met one person who jubilantly says bring on the correction; I'm up for it. Most of us resent the method or the person who corrected us and in our embarrassment can miss the error we have made. Age is not a qualifier, Jared at 3 didn't like it, and Grandma at 103 didn't like it either.

But there is an even greater pearl of wisdom than that one. I learned that people often try to understand a concept without really taking the time to learn what is involved. He was 3, had never seen a cow, and had never seen a coyote. He was in way over his head. His conclusion was pretty good for someone who had no idea what we were talking about.

Sometimes you can get away with it. Take football (soccer) for example! It is pretty straightforward; lots of men on the field with a goal at each end. Must be two teams as the majority of them are wearing one of two jerseys. Then there are the funny guys with the really odd outfits standing by the goal, maybe the goalie. Obviously you want one team to put the ball in the other teams goal. How hard can it be? If a person falls down, grabbing his shin, then make all the man noises as if you are upset. Somebody will be upset that either he's faking it, or it's for real. All you have to do is be upset and follow the crowd to get the consensus of what went wrong. Don't go against the flow and whose the wiser?

It worked well for my uncle while watching North American football. He really didn't have a clue what was going on but hey, he's a man's man. Drinking beer with my father and shooting the bull was all he needed. Unfortunately he didn't know about instant replay. The opposition had scored against our hometown team with a beautiful pass and long run.

The replay came on and my uncle jumped up all excited. "My God, look, look, look! The b----------ds did it again."

My dad just smiled and didn't say anything. How many people are just smiling at us and saying nothing?

40 NINJA STARS

The farm had a building we called the barn but was really a work shed for the cedar lumber business. We had a selection of tools including radial arm saw, table saw, planer and a grinder. The grinder was Grandpa's particular favorite. He loved running the disks over the axes, knives and generally anything with a blade that needed sharpening. It was the most dramatic of the tools in that it left off this beautiful shower of sparks when the metal contacted the grinding wheel. The kids loved it. Grandpa gave the older boys strict orders to stay away from it, as it was too dangerous for them to handle.

Might as well hold a red rag up to a bull as tell two boys 8 and 9 not to touch a power tool. They used to get the lids off the tin cans in the recycling, sneak into the barn and cut out Ninja stars, sharpening the edges to fine razor sharpness. I never caught them at this and they didn't confess to it until 20 years later. Even in their confession their eyes lit up and you could see the two of them at that age again. "Wow! They really flew and sliced into the wood!"

Is it too late for me to learn anything from it? Probably but thank God they survived. The lesson for any parent is no matter how much you shelter your children they will try what you forbid, especially if you enjoy it yourself. They eventually see that as hypocrisy and absolutely have to try it. If you don't believe in God, when you have children, it's a good time to start. Angels around them is a necessary requirement for surviving childhood.

Also children will be less curious about what concerns you if you are more open about issues. A friend of mine when his children were under 5 years of age went to Africa where he met a missionary. She was a chocoholic and a compulsive cola and coffee drinker. Her parents were very strict about what she could and couldn't have growing up. They were concerned that she only eat and drink what they thought was healthy. Now in her 30s she could not control her desires for those products. Previously to this visit my friend had taken the same stand with his wife and children. But when he returned, he gave chocolates to each of his girls and his wife a bag of coffee. He didn't want his children to end up like this woman.

Another man I knew had been forbidden as a child to read the color comics in the Saturday paper. It was his weekly chore to get to the paper first, take the comics out and burn them before any of his siblings could see them. In his 30s he had no idea of what was appropriate or inappropriate to watch. He watched videos with his young children that were rated as suitable for adults only. He didn't want his children to feel that they had missed out on something in their childhood. In his adverse reaction to his parents he had swung so far to the opposite position that he was exposing his children to images that were damaging to their little minds. He had no control and no discernment.

When Joel was 16, he told us that he was going to dye his hair blue. We said, "That's fine, it'll look good." He shook his head and said we took all the fun out of trying to be rebellious. He didn't dye his hair either. Forbidding is the hook that creates desire for the fruit. 'No' or 'don't' create a strong desire in people to do just the opposite. The human race does not like to be told what to do, especially if something appears pleasant to them. It is better to express your concerns for your children's safety to them, or if the situation is appropriate explain you will do it with them or acknowledge that it is fun and possible under the proper guidelines, i.e., age appropriate. They will trust you and your word that you are protecting them not withholding something that you enjoy but refuse them.

41 CONCLUSION

I took an oil painting lesson not long ago. At the end of our session where the instructor and I had completed a painting he said to me a painting is never finished. Because of that he said the key to knowing it is complete is to watch for when you start fussing with details and adding just one more thing. I feel that way now about this book. Should I add one more incident? Should I add many more? Is it sufficient? Maybe I should tweak this chapter or that one?

I could go on with more incidents and more thoughts stemming from them. But rather than keep fussing I think for now it is done.

I hope this wee book has inspired you to look at life afresh, to stop and smell the flowers. If there is anything I have learned over the years it is to stop rushing to the next goal or event. You can miss so much of what is happening today that is good and wholesome and encouraging. The frustration of trying to get something else or somewhere else can rob you of the joy of life. At the end of life how many people say, 'Oh, I wish I had spent more time at the office?'

Planning is great. Planning is exciting. But living in the future can steal away all of your todays. The tension of life is to balance what is, what was and what is to come. Any swing to one in preference to the others will cause you to lose the joy of life. We can't always be looking back or we will walk into a metaphorical wall. We can't live only for the now as our decisions may be rash and irresponsible. We can't always plan for tomorrow, as we will miss all that is good and valuable today.

When I was fifteen I suffered from a ruptured appendix. I was two weeks in the hospital and two weeks at home before I could return to school. The monotony of the enforced confinement, the lack of things to do, the physical restrains due to the operation and the need to recover all developed an appreciation within me for simple things in life. The joy of a walk or being able to run, the freedom to come and go when and where I pleased, the pleasure of having people to interact with, and even the appreciation of having a teacher explain concepts were all new found delights that I had taken for granted until this setback. The saying there is a silver lining in every cloud is true if you look for it. Life is precious. I hope you will be inspired to appreciate the moments more through reading Eyes of Wonder.

May your eyes of wonder be re-opened!

ABOUT THE AUTHOR

Jim is a spiritual entrepreneur. He has asked the question "Why can't we?" throughout his Christian walk. Over and over the Lord has answered "yes, you can." Jim has pastored churches, planted churches, started leadership colleges, co-pioneered a church movement, developed marriage and parenting seminars with his lovely wife, Bonnie. Together they wrote 24 Secrets to Great Parenting.

Jim is an author and international speaker. He has a Father's heart and has four wonderful children of his own and a great many spiritual children.

His greatest passion is to teach others how to "do the stuff" of the Kingdom of God. 2 Timothy 2:2, "And the things you have heard me say in the presence of many witnesses entrust to reliable men who will also be qualified to teach others", has been his life's inspiration.

OTHER BOOKS AND RESOURCES BY JIM INKSTER
The Heart of the Matter
(paperback)

The Heart of the Matter is an interesting journey into the heart of God and our response to His amazing unconditional giving. It reveals excellent revelation and insight into the heart of our heavenly Father.

Available through Amazon and Kindle

OTHER BOOKS AND RESOURCES BY JIM AND BONNIE INKSTER

24 Secrets To Great Parenting
(paperback)

Jim and Bonnie share from their vast experience the principles that helped them raise four great children. It is written in a light-hearted, easy reading style perfect for the busy parent with very little spare time on their hands.

Available through Amazon and on Kindle.

8 Questions Every Parent Wants Answered (DVD)

Jim and Bonnie surveyed hundreds of parents to find what issues are their greatest concern regarding their children. Eight questions were consistent from parents throughout the world.

These questions have been addressed in a powerful and entertaining format. Each session takes less than 10 minutes with great ideas for successful application within your family.

Available through Amazon.
24 Secrets to Great Parenting
(audiobook)

Jim and Bonnie felt that this great book had to be available to everyone including those who don't like to read. The research shows men prefer to listen, women prefer to read.

Jim was professionally studio recorded reading this charming and helpful book. Great for in the car or on your personal player when exercising or simply chilling.

OTHER BOOKS AND RESOURCES BY JIM AND BONNIE INKSTER

The Christmas Story

Great Blogs

www.jimandbonnie.co.uk

Jim and Bonnie write a weekly blog giving thoughtful and sometimes witty insights into relationships, marriage and parenting.

Don't miss it!

www.gatewaysministries.com

www.jimandbonnieinkster.com

Jim and Bonnie can be contacted through these websites.

www.ingramcontent.com/pod-product-compliance
Lightning Source LLC
LaVergne TN
LVHW051602070426
835507LV00021B/2724